Thomas Francis Moran

The Rise and Development of the Bicameral System in

America

Thomas Francis Moran

The Rise and Development of the Bicameral System in America

ISBN/EAN: 9783337036003

Printed in Europe, USA, Canada, Australia, Japan

Cover: Foto ©Suzi / pixelio.de

More available books at **www.hansebooks.com**

JOHNS HOPKINS UNIVERSITY STUDIES

IN

HISTORICAL AND POLITICAL SCIENCE

HERBERT B. ADAMS, Editor.

History is Past Politics and Politics are Present History—*Freeman.*

THIRTEENTH SERIES

V

THE RISE AND DEVELOPMENT

OF THE

BICAMERAL SYSTEM IN AMERICA

By THOMAS FRANCIS MORAN, A. B.,

Fellow in History, J. H. U.

BALTIMORE

THE JOHNS HOPKINS PRESS

PUBLISHED MONTHLY

MAY, 1895.

CONTENTS.

THE RISE AND DEVELOPMENT OF THE BICAMERAL SYSTEM IN AMERICA.

INTRODUCTION.

The purpose of this study is to trace the rise and development of the bicameral system from its beginnings in Massachusetts to its incorporation into the Federal Constitution. The acknowledged importance and universal application of this principle of government would seem to warrant a study of the various steps and, in so far as may be, of the causes which led to its introduction into the federal and all of the state constitutions. It is not necessary at this late day to exalt the importance of the bicameral principle. "The division of the legislature into two separate and independent branches," says Kent, "is founded on such obvious principles of good policy, and is so strongly recommended by the unequivocal language of experience, that it has obtained the general approbation of the people of this country." [1] It is, however, no part of the object of this paper to discuss the advantages or disadvantages of the system. Its philosophic aspects have attracted the attention of Kent,[2] Story,[3] Lieber [4] and a host of other political writers of eminence both in Europe and America. With this phase of the subject we have nothing to do. It is to the historical evolution of the system that we turn our attention.

---

[1] Commentaries, I, Sec. 222. [2] *Ibid.*, Secs. 222–224.
[3] Commentaries, II, 26–45.
[4] Civil Liberty and Self Government, Chap. XVII. See also John Adams' Defence of the American Constitutions.

7

CHAPTER I.

The New England Colonies.

Section I.—Massachusetts.

In tracing the rise and development of the bicameral system in America, we naturally begin our study with Massachusetts, since it is here that we first find a colonial legislature consisting of two houses. In 1629 a charter was granted in England to the "Governor and Company of Mattachusetts Bay in Newe-England." In the following year the company and their charter were transferred to America. In accordance with this patent the whole body of freemen elected annually a governor, deputy-governor, and eighteen assistants[1] for "ordering of the generall buysines and Affaires." The legislative power, however, resided in the general assembly of freemen. The freemen met four times a year for the purpose of enacting laws. This plan soon seemed impracticable, and, in October, 1630, the power of electing governor and deputy-governor and of enacting laws was given to the assistants. The number of assistants actually performing the functions of their office was at times as low as five. Here, then, was an incipient oligarchy. The natural result followed. This vast power could not be placed in the hands of a privileged few with impunity. In performing their functions of office it became necessary for the assistants to levy a tax. In 1631 the people of Watertown refused to pay the tax thus levied on the ground that it was "taxation without representation." The pastor, elder, and a

---

[1] Poore's *Charters and Constitutions*, I, 932.

8

few leading members of the Watertown church, when summoned before the Governor and assistants, declared that " it was not safe to pay moneys after that sort, for fear of bringing themselves and posterity into bondage." [1] They further say that they consider the government " no other but as of a mayor and aldermen, who have not power to make laws or raise taxations without the people." The assistants reply that the government is " rather in the nature of a parliament," and that the assistants, being chosen by the freemen, are their legal representatives, and so vested with power to levy taxes. The Watertown men concede the point, make a written apology for their obstinacy, and, according to the Journal of Governor Winthrop, go home apparently satisfied. Yet this protest, though apparently of no avail, was the origin of a very important constitutional change. The train of ideas thus set in motion led to the introduction of the representative system in 1632.[2] In May of that year each town chose two deputies to meet in the General Court with the Governor and assistants and to advise with them with regard to the raising of a " publique stocke." [3] We have here an analogue of the English Parliament. In this humble legislative Assembly the germs of the bicameral system are plainly discernible. The assistants were elected by the people at large while the deputies were chosen by the various towns. This difference in the modes of election naturally led both to think of themselves as constituting two separate bodies, though they deliberated and voted as one. What was to be their real status? Were they

---

[1] Winthrop's *History of New England*, I, p. 84 (Savage's edition).

[2] Neither in the Massachusetts Records nor Gov. Winthrop's Journal is there any expressed connection between the Watertown case and the introduction of the representative system, yet the general drift of the matter indicates that such must have been the case. Doyle, in speaking of the introduction of the representative system says: " We can hardly err in supposing that this was the direct result of the protest made by the men of Watertown." *Puritan Cols.*, Vol. I, 106.

[3] Winthrop, I, 91; Massachusetts Records, I, 95.

to continue to deliberate and to vote as a single body, which they outwardly were, or as two separate bodies, which they were in reality? The charter made no provision for the body of deputies, hence their relation to the assistants was not defined. The question was therefore left for decision to the unwritten law of the constitution and was decided in accordance with English precedent with which the colonists were of course familiar. The test case was not long in presenting itself. It came in 1634. In September of that year the people of Newtown (now Cambridge) asked the permission of the General Court to remove to Connecticut. Their principal reason for moving was that they might have more land for pasturage. This request naturally met with some opposition. When the matter came to a vote the Governor, fifteen deputies, and two assistants voted to grant the request, while the Deputy-Governor, ten deputies, and "the rest of the assistants" voted to deny it.[1] The number of assistants voting upon the question was probably seven; hence a majority of the deputies voted in the affirmative, a majority of the assistants in the negative, and a majority (18 out of 34) of the entire Court, if taken as a single body, in the affirmative. The deputies claimed that the motion was carried, while the assistants held that it was lost. The protest of the assistants was entered "because there were not six assistants in the vote, as the patent" required.[2] A deadlock ensued and business was brought to a stand-still. In order to solve the perplexing

---

[1] Winthrop, I, 168; Barry's *History of Massachusetts*, I, 273-4.

[2] Winthrop, I, 168. This provision was contained in the charter. (Poore, *Charters and Constitutions*, I, 937). The charter, however, was somewhat modified by later legislation of the General Court. Provision was made in the patent for eighteen assistants, but up to 1640 their number did not exceed twelve. Seven of the assistants were constituted a quorum by the charter; but in March, 1631, after some of them had returned to England, the General Court resolved that when there were fewer than nine assistants in the colony a majority of the number so present should constitute a quorum and that their acts should be as binding as if the full number of seven or more were present. Massachusetts Records, I, 84.

problem a day of fasting, humiliation, and prayer was observed ; and, after a sermon upon the subject by the Rev. John Cotton, "the affairs of the court went on cheerfully."[1] The assistants carried their point and made good their claim, in this instance at least, to a negative upon the acts of the deputies. The victory was not a signal one, however. The turn which matters now took in the Newtown case no doubt diverted attention from the real point at issue and aided the assistants in sustaining their claim. Boston and Watertown ceded some of their land to Newtown[2] and the main cause, certainly the alleged one, for removal was taken away. Although the Newtown case was thus disposed of and a precedent established in favor of a negative on the part of the assistants, the relations between the two bodies were not definitely settled and a clashing of authority was inevitable. Finally in 1636 the General Court pronounced upon the matter in the following terms :

"And whereas it may fall out that in some of theis Genall Courts, to be holden by the magistrates & deputies, there may arise some difference of judgem^t in doubtfull cases, it is therefore ordered, that noe lawe, order, or sentence shall passe as an act of the Court, without the consent of the great^r p̄te of the magistrates on the one p̄te, & the great^r number of the deputyes on the other p̄te ; . . ."[3]

This act rendered the two bodies coördinate in legislative authority and introduced one of the most essential features of the bicameral system. They continued to sit together, however, until 1644. The immediate cause of their separation was the famous case of Mrs. Sherman's pig, or, as dignified old Governor Hutchinson puts it, the "controversy between the two houses at this time was occasioned by a difference in sentiment upon the identity of a swine which was claimed by a poor woman as

---

[1] Winthrop, I, 169.
[2] Massachusetts Records, I, 129 ; Winthrop, I, 169.
[3] Massachusetts Records, Vol. I, p. 170.

having strayed from her some years before, and, her title being disputed by a person of more consequence, divided not the court only, but the whole country." [1]   The case was brought for final hearing to the General Court and the controversy was much more animated than the matter at issue would seem to deserve.   Fifteen deputies and two assistants were favorable to Mrs. Sherman, while eight deputies and seven assistants espoused the cause of Captain Keayne.   Seven assistants refrained from voting.   As an outcome of the controversy the General Court resolved that the two bodies should sit apart, that bills might originate in either, and that a bill having passed one house should go to the other for "assent or dissent." Bills passed by both houses were to be "ingrossed" and "read deliberately" on the last day of the session before final assent was given.   The reasons assigned by the General Court for the above resolution were that "divers inconveniences" resulted from the sitting together of the two bodies, and that they accounted it the part of "wisdome to follow the laudable practice of other states who have layd groundworks for government & order." [2]   We have here a conscious and avowed reversion to English precedent.   As Professor Fisher justly remarks, "the form of government was now assimilated to the English model." [3]

William C. Morey, in speaking of the bicameral system, says : "It would be difficult to imagine how any institution could be regarded as more indigenous to the soil or more completely shaped by the peculiar circumstances of time and place than was this system as it took its rise in Massachusetts." [4] The system was certainly "shaped by the peculiar circumstances of time and place," but can hardly be called "indigenous to the soil."   The system in its growth and development,

---

[1] Hutchinson's *History of Massachusetts*, I, 135.   (Ed. of 1795.)

[2] Massachusetts Records, II, 58-9.

[3] Colonial Era, 113.

[4] Annals of the American Academy of Political and Social Science, Sept. 1893, p. 13.

as typified by the case of Massachusetts, was essentially American; but the bicameral principle did not originate on this side of the Atlantic, and the development of the institution in America was directly influenced, as we have seen, by the English model. The charter under which the colony was founded was not a complete scheme of government and it was repeatedly enlarged and modified by enactments of the General Court. Such modifications are scarcely ever made, and certainly were not in this case, with unanimity. When confronted with such constitutional questions the people of Massachusetts made such application of English precedent and English custom as seemed suited to the exigencies of the occasion. When the people of Watertown refused to pay the tax on the ground that they had no direct representation in the government, the matter was adjusted, after some delay, by introducing a system of town representation. Again, the bicameral system was resorted to as a solution of the difficulties attending the Newtown case and the case of Sherman *v.* Keayne. It seems entirely probable that these great principles of government would, sooner or later, have found their way into the American system regardless of English precedent; but it is also clear that the familiarity of the colonists with the practical working of these institutions in England hastened their introduction into American legislatures. It must be borne in mind that these men were Englishmen and imbued with English political ideas; and, although many of them had left England to escape persecution, they still believed the English government to be the best in the world, and hated, not the government itself, but its administration in the hands of the Stuarts.

Section II.—New Hampshire.

Although the colony of New Hampshire was founded at a comparatively early period, it was not until 1679 that she set out upon an independent governmental career. Up to this date the New Hampshire settlements consisting of the four towns of Portsmouth, Hampton, Dover, and Exeter, were under the jurisdiction of Massachusetts. On September 18, 1679, however, a royal commission [1] was issued by Charles II constituting New Hampshire a separate province and naming for her a president and council. John Cutts [2] was named in this document as president,[3] and a council of six was designated—three from Portsmouth, and one from each of the remaining towns. The President and Council were authorized to appoint three additional councillors,[4] and were instructed to summon a general assembly. All laws passed by this assembly were to be submitted to the President and Council for approval and then sent to England for final approval or rejection.[5] The President was empowered to recommend to the Assembly the passage of any laws which he thought conducive to the general welfare of the colony. The first General Assembly under this frame of government convened on March 16, 1680, at Portsmouth.[6] At this meeting, as at all subsequent ones, joint sessions excepted, the two branches, following the evident intention of the commission, sat apart.[7] The temper of the people regarding their legislative prerogatives is plainly discernible in an act passed at this session by the Assembly and approved by the President and Council. It was enacted that " no Act, Imposition, Law or Ordinance be made or imposed upon " the people " but such as shall be made by the said Assembly and approved by the Presid[t] and Councill."[8] It is clear that the representative Assembly was determined to assert itself as a very important factor in legislation. Provision was made for meetings of the General Assembly to

---

[1] New Hampshire Provincial Papers, I, 373; Poore, *Charters and Constitutions*, II, 1275.

[2] He is called Cutt in the Commission.

[3] Prov. Papers, I, 374.   [4] *Ibid.*, 375.

[5] *Ibid.*, 379–80.   [6] *Ibid.*, 382.

[7] See Belknap's *History of New Hampshire*, I, 178–9; also Farmer's Belknap's *Hist. of N. H.*, 453.

[8] Prov. Papers, I, 382–3; Farmer's Belknap, 453–4.

be held annually at Portsmouth, on the first Tuesday in March.[1]

President Cutts died in 1682, and, after a short interval, was succeeded by Edward Cranfield. His commission[2] of May 9, 1682, authorized him " to make, constitute, and ordain laws, statutes and ordinances " " by and with the advice and consent of" the Council and Assembly, "or the major part of them respectively." A council of ten members was named in the commission and the Governor was given a negative on all laws. It is evident from the language above quoted from the commission that the intention was to continue the bicameral system in the legislature. This was done.[3] The Assembly, however, was almost a nonentity during the iniquitous administration of Cranfield. Owing to a disagreement it was dissolved by the Governor in 1683, and the legislative power was assumed by the Governor and Council.[4] Being in want of money the Governor summoned another Assembly, which met on January 14, 1684. He submitted to them a money bill which was drawn up and previously passed by the Council. This method of originating money bills was deemed " unparliamentary " by the popular representatives, and the bill was promptly rejected. The Assembly was just as promptly dissolved, January 15.[5] Another Assembly called in July of the same year was almost immediately dissolved, and was the last one in Cranfield's administration.[6]

Under the rule of Andros laws were enacted by the Governor and Council without the aid of a popular assembly. On April 18, 1689, after the news of the deposition of King James and the coronation of William and Mary reached New Hampshire, Andros was called upon to surrender the govern-

---

[1] Prov. Papers, I, 395.	[2] *Ibid.*, 433.

[3] See Belknap, I, 193. " No *Journal of the House* separate from the joint Journal of the Council and Assembly is found till 1711." Bouton in preface to Prov. Papers, Vol. III, pt. II.

[4] Belknap, I, 201.	[5] *Ibid.*, 203–4.

[6] *Ibid.*, 214.

ment.[1] From this time until 1692 affairs were in a decidedly unsettled condition.[2] Finally, on March 1, 1692, a commission[3] was issued to Samuel Allen designating him as Governor. This commission and the instructions[4] issued on March 7 of the same year constituted a frame of government the legislative department of which differed in no way from that provided for in the commission and instructions of Governor Cranfield. The names of a council of ten members appear in the instructions. It was the evident intention that the two houses should sit apart and constitute two coördinate branches of the legislature. That they did so in actual practice is evident from an inspection of the records.[5]

The constitution of January 5, 1776, provided for a legislature consisting of a House of Representatives and a Council. The two branches were to be distinct and coördinate.[6]

Section III.—Connecticut.

In Connecticut the development of the bicameral system took place not as a consequence of the jealousy existing between the parts of the legislative body, as was the case in Massachusetts, but was due to a large extent to the harmonious relations existing between the assistants and deputies.

According to the *Fundamental Orders*[7] of January 14, 1639, the legislative body, called the General Assembly or General Court, was to consist of the Governor, magistrates, and four deputies from each of the confederating towns.[8] The magistrates were elected by the whole body of freemen and the deputies by the people of the respective towns. The magis-

---

[1] Prov. Papers, II, pt. I, 21.   [2] *Ibid.*, II, pt. I, 30.
[3] *Ibid.*, II, pt. I, 57.   [4] *Ibid.*, II, pt. I, 63.
[5] See Minutes of the Council in Prov. Papers, II, pt. I, 109 ff.; also Journal of Council and Assembly in Prov. Papers, III, pt. II, 5 ff.
[6] Charters and Constitutions, II, 1279–80.
[7] *Ibid.*, I, 249.
[8] Windsor, Hartford and Wethersfield.

trates and deputies composed one house and were presided over by the Governor, who, in case of a tie, cast the deciding vote. The deputies were, however, authorized to meet by themselves at some time previous to the meeting of the General Assembly "to aduise and consult of all such things as may concerne the good of the publike."[1] This fact together with the different modes of election seems to foreshadow the further differentiation of functions and the eventual separation of the two bodies.

The *Fundamental Orders* were succeeded by the charter of 1662.[2] It was this charter which the younger Winthrop was sent to secure and in the negotiation of which he was so eminently successful. The King evidently gave him all he asked for, and, as a consequence, this charter left little to be desired. In the language of Professor Johnston, it "raised the Connecticut leaders to the seventh heaven of satisfaction."[3] It was practically a confirmation of the *Fundamental Orders* with two changes of importance, both of which were desired by the colonists. The number of deputies was changed to two and the Colony of New Haven was included. The latter provision was as agreeable to Connecticut as it was odious to New Haven. The charter provided for a legislative body,—a governor or deputy-governor, twelve assistants, and a number of deputies not exceeding two from each "Place, Town, or City." The Governor, Deputy-Governor, and assistants were to be chosen by the whole body of freemen in primary assembly, while the deputies were to be elected by the people of their respective localities. All constituted one house, and that they dwelt together in peace and harmony—a condition of things quite unusual in colonial legislatures—is evidenced by a resolution of the General Court of 1678. In May of that year the Governor, Deputy-Governor, and assistants were constituted a "standing councill to issue all such occasions and matters as"

---

[1] Charters and Constitutions, I, 251.
[2] *Ibid.*, 252–7.
[3] Genesis of a New England State, Johns Hopkins University Studies, Vol. I, No. 11, p. 26.

should "fall in in the intervalls of the Generall Court." [1] As the regular meetings of the Court took place in May and October, such a standing committee seemed a necessity. This resolution is an important step in the separation of the two bodies. It was, as Professor Johnston has remarked, "the prelude to the inevitable introduction of a bi-cameral system." [2] The confidence thus reposed in the assistants seems not to have been abused, for the authority conferred upon them in 1678 was regularly continued at the May and October meetings of the Court until 1686. At this time there arose a complication of affairs which placed matters of the gravest importance in the hands of the Governor and Council. Under date of May 27, 1686, Edward Randolph, a royal commissioner and forerunner of Edmund Andros, wrote to Governor Treat and Council asking them to surrender their charter. He said that a writ of *quo warranto* had been issued against Connecticut, and that he had been intrusted with the serving of it. He would greatly prefer, however, he said, to have the people of Connecticut gain royal favor by a voluntary surrender of their charter before the service of the writ. He proclaimed the intention of the King as being "to bring all New England under one Governem^t," and boldly asserted that nothing remained for the people of Connecticut but "an humble submission and dutifull resignation" of their charter. He counselled haste in the matter. "S^{rs}," said he, "bless not yourselues wth vaine expectation of advantage & spinninge out of time by my delay : I will engage tho' the weather be warme the writs will keep sound and as good as when first landed." [3]

---

[1] Colonial Records of Conn., 1678–1689, p. 15.

[2] Connecticut, 269.

[3] Letter of Edward Randolph to Gov. Treat and Council, in Colonial Records of Conn., 1678–1689, pp. 352-4.

The writs would certainly be as sound and as good as when first landed, for they were even then perfectly worthless. Randolph's voyage was an unusually long one—about six months in duration—and the time for the return of the writs had expired before he reached America.

Governor Treat and his Councillors, however, were decidedly of the opinion that something did remain aside from " humble submission " and " dutifull resignation." A meeting of the Council was accordingly called, and on June 11, 1686, an answer was drafted and sent to Mr. Randolph. In this emergency the Governor called a special session of the General Court for July 6, 1686. He reported the action taken by himself and Council upon the receipt of Mr. Randolph's letter, and that action was approved.[1]

This Randolph episode was a very important incident in the development of the bicameral system. Heretofore, the business transacted by the Council in the recesses of the General Court was largely of a routine character, and report upon it was not deemed essential ; but in this case, when the very liberties of the colony were at stake, Governor Treat and Council deemed it wise and expedient to lay the whole matter before the General Court in special session and ask their endorsement. This was the beginning of a system of report and approval whereby all important matters passed upon by the Governor and Council were reviewed by the entire Court. This custom was, too, an important step toward the separate voting and separate deliberation of the two bodies.

After approving the action of the Council the General Court appointed that body a committee to prepare an address upon the matter to the King.[2]

Mr. Randolph, finding but cold comfort in the resolute replies of the Council, served the writ on July 20–21, at midnight. Another extra session of the Court was deemed necessary and was called for July 28, 1686. At this meeting the Governor and Council were instructed to appoint an agent to represent the colony in England.[3] Mr. William Whiting, a London merchant, was accordingly commissioned to act in this capacity. At the next meeting of the Court this action

---

[1] Colonial Records of Connecticut, 1678–1689, p. 208.
[2] *Ibid.*, p. 208. [3] *Ibid.*, 213.

was reported to that body and approved by it.[1] The weighty matters with which the Council was now dealing and the general colonial aversion toward anything savoring of unrestricted authority combined to render this method of report and approval a popular one.

Andros landed December 20, 1686, and demanded the surrender of the charter. A special session of the Court convened on January 26, 1687, and the Council was again empowered to take such action as seemed wise and expedient.[2] The outcome of the matter is well known. Andros governed as viceroy from 1687 to his expulsion, in April of 1689. In the interim charter government was, of course, suspended.

Immediately after the resumption of charter government in 1689, steps were taken toward making it obligatory upon the Council to submit certain of their acts to the General Court for approval. In May of 1689, the deputies expressed their desire by vote that all matters concerning the "charter or government" should be decided by the General Court, in special session if need be, and not left to the independent action of the Council.[3] This advice was soon acted upon by the Court. The custom which obtained before the viceroyalty of Andros of constituting the Governor and Council a standing committee for the transaction of business in the recesses of the General Court was continued, but was modified in one essential particular: it was now definitely and repeatedly stated that there were certain matters with which the Council was not to deal. Naturally enough the matters thus sacredly guarded had to do with their charter liberties and the levying of taxes. In October of 1691, the General Court, after conferring the usual authority upon the Council, added the proviso that they (the Council) "rayse no money nor make no alteration of o[r] charter government."[4] In October of 1692, it is likewise

---

[1] Colonial Records of Connecticut, 1678–1689, pp. 217–218.
[2] *Ibid.*, p. 226.   [3] *Ibid.*, 252–3.   [4] *Ibid.*, 1689–1706, p. 62.

" provided [that] they doe not intermeddle with the altering
or parting with any of our charter rights and priviledges
without the consent and appoyntment of our Generall Court." [1]
Again in October, 1697, the same restriction is placed upon
the acts of the Council.[2] This custom marks another step
in the evolution of the bicameral system.

It is noticeable that during the period between 1689 and
1698 the acts of the Council, even those not relating to taxes
and the charter, were submitted with greater frequency and
regularity to the General Court for approval.[3] In 1698, however, instead of approving isolated acts of the Council a general
approval was expressed in the following terms : " This Court
declared their approbation of what hath been acted by the
Council since Octob[r] last." [4] This substitution of general for
specific approval marks another step in the process of the
separation of the two bodies. The Council in the meantime
still continued to serve the colony in various capacities. In
April of 1690 that body was appointed a " Councill of War,"
and two years later was commissioned to try several persons
" indicted for familiarity with Satan." [5] Duties of far more
importance from a legislative standpoint, and of peculiar interest in our present study, devolved upon the Council in 1698.
In May of that year they were instructed to make an inquiry
as to the extent to which the laws of England were in force
in America and to report the result to the General Court.
They were also instructed *to prepare and report bills* for the
regulation of courts of justice, to suggest proper methods of
raising revenue, and to devise a plan for the suppression of
vice.[6] This process of legislation approximates very closely
the essential features of the bicameral system, and little was
wanting to make the evolution of that system complete. The

---

[1] Colonial Records of Connecticut, 1689–1706, pp. 84–5.
[2] *Ibid.*, 226.   [3] See *Ibid.*, pp. 47, 149, 202, 205.
[4] *Ibid.*, 251.   [5] See *Ibid.*, pp. 76, 102, 205.
[6] *Ibid.*, 261–2.

final step in the process was taken in October of 1698, and is thus recorded : " It is ordered by this Court and the author   tye thereof, that for the future this Gener^ll Assembly shall consist of two houses ; the first shall consist of the Govern^r or, in his absence, of the Deputye Govern^r, and Assistants, which shall be known by the name of the Upper House ; the other shall consist of such Deputies as shall be legally returned from the severall towns within this Colonie, to serve as members of this Generall Assembly, which shall be known by the name of the Lower House, wherein a Speaker chosen by themselves shall preside : which houses so formed shall have a distinct power to appoint all needfull officers, and to make such rules as they shall severally judge necessary for the regulating of themselves. And it is further ordered that no act shall be passed into a law of this Colonie, nor any law already enacted be repealed, nor any other act proper to this Generall Assembly but by the consent of both houses." [1]

Section IV.—Rhode Island.

Although agitation for the separation of the two branches was begun at a very early period on the part of the deputies, more than a half century elapsed between the granting of the first charter and the introduction of the bicameral system. This long delay was, in large part, due to the peculiar method of its introduction, and particularly to a compromise upon the matter between the magistrates and deputies in May, 1668.

The English Parliamentary Commission granted a charter or patent to the Providence Plantations on March 14, 1644. The first General Assembly was held at Portsmouth, May 19–21, 1647. At this Assembly the charter, an exceedingly liberal one, was adopted, and the government systematically organized. A majority of the freemen of the colony were

---

[1] Colonial Records of Connecticut, 1689–1706, p. 267.

present and declared forty a quorum to do business.[1]   Thus
early do we find the germ of the representative system in the
government of the new colony.[2]

The charter of 1663 vested the government of the colony
in a governor, deputy-governor, ten assistants, and eighteen
deputies.[3]   As in Connecticut, the Governor, Deputy-Governor,
and assistants were chosen annually by the entire body of the
freemen, while the deputies were elected by the people of the
respective towns.[4]   Here as in Connecticut the different modes

---

[1] Colonial Records of Rhode Island, I, 147.

[2] See Arnold's *History of Rhode Island,* I, 201-2.
The method devised by this Assembly for the passing of laws was a
curious mixture of the representative system and the referendum.   Any
town of the colony—Providence, Portsmouth, Newport or Warwick—could
initiate legislation.   When a town desired the passage of a certain law, the
matter was discussed and voted upon in the town-meeting.   In case of an
affirmative vote, a copy of the bill was sent to each of the other towns to be
debated and determined in like manner.   A report of the action taken by
the various towns was then referred to a "Committee for the General
Courte" consisting of six members from each town.   This committee, acting
as a central canvassing board, determined whether or not the proposed
measure had been sanctioned by the "Major parte of the Colonie."   If so,
the matter was declared a law to stand until the next meeting of the General Assembly.   The final disposition of the matter was then made.   It was,
in short, the duty of the committee to promulgate laws, not to pass them.
The initiative in legislation was, however, given to them to be exercised in
this way.   They were authorized to discuss and determine among themselves
any matter presented to them that might "be deemed necessary for the
public weale and good of the whole."   The various members then reported
the action of the committee to their respective towns, by whom it was
discussed and voted upon.   The votes were sealed and forwarded to the
General Recorder of the colony to be opened and counted in the presence
of the President.   In case it was found that the proposition had received a
majority vote, it was declared a law to stand until the next meeting of the
General Assembly, by which it was either confirmed or rejected.   Colonial
Records of Rhode Island, I, 148-9.   See also Arnold's *History of Rhode Island,*
I, 203.

[3] Newport was allowed six deputies, and the remaining towns four each.
It was also provided that any town subsequently added should have two
deputies.

[4] Charters and Constitutions, II, 1597-1599.   Colonial Records of Rhode
Island, II, 7-11.

of election constitute the germ of the bicameral system ; and, though all sat in the same house, the time was not far distant when separation was to be sought.　It is evident from the records that steps looking toward this end were taken almost immediately.　It was recorded in October of 1664, that there had "been a long agetation about the motion whether the magistrates [assistants]" should "sitt by themselves and the deputyes by themselves."[1]　The matter was put over to the next meeting of the Assembly.　It appears that this "long agetation" was caused by petitions from Warwick and Portsmouth asking for the separation of the two bodies.　No further action seems to have been taken until March of 1666. The petitions of the two towns were now duly discussed, and after "haveing well weighed such conveniances" and "inconveniancyes" as might result from the separation, the Assembly decided to grant the request, and accordingly ordered that the deputies and assistants should sit apart.　The settling of the details of the change was put over to the meeting of the following May.[2]　At that time, however, no action was taken owing to the small attendance of the deputies.　In September the Assembly seemed undecided as to the advisability of the change and ordered the temporary suspension of the enactment by which the separation of the two bodies was to have been effected.　All members of the Assembly thus continued to constitute one house.[3]　In October of the same year (1666), a definite decision was reached.　At this time the Assembly, "having had long and serious debates about the premises," ordered that the two bodies should constitute one house as heretofore until further action be taken.[4]

It is not at all strange that at this time the debate upon the merits of the bicameral system should have been "long and serious," inasmuch as it had not fully demonstrated its applicability to American conditions, and certainly was not

---

[1] Colonial Records of Rhode Island, II, 63.　　[3] *Ibid.*, 144–5.
[2] *Ibid.*, 150–1.　　　　　　　　　　　[4] *Ibid.*, 181.

then what De Tocqueville afterwards termed it—"an axiom in the political science of the present age." [1]

In May, 1667, the Governor and Council began a series of frequent meetings [2] to dispose of important matters arising in the intervals of the General Court. The hostility of the French and Dutch together with the surly mutterings of Indian enmity which culminated in King Philip's War rendered this a critical period in the existence of the new colony. These separate meetings served to differentiate further the functions of the two bodies.

The agitation for the final separation of the two bodies seems to have gone steadily on; and in May, 1668, it resulted in a compromise which was destined to delay the introduction of the bicameral system in its complete form for nearly three decades. At this time the deputies requested that they be allowed to withdraw from the Assembly "to consider of such affaires as they may think fitt to propose for the well beinge of the Collony." This request was granted, but with the proviso that they return to the Assembly in half an hour. It was further enacted that the same permission be accorded the deputies in the future in case a majority of them should desire it. No law was to be passed in their absence. [3]

In 1672 a method which still quite meets the approval of politicians was resorted to in order to allay the jealousy arising between the two bodies. The Treasurer was instructed to provide, at public expense, a dinner "ffor the keepinge of the Magistrates and Deputies in love together, for the ripeninge of their consultations, and husbandinge of their time." [4]

Although as a result of various compromises and devices the deputies continued to sit in the same chamber with the magistrates, it is clear that certainly as early as 1672 they looked upon themselves as a separate and distinct body. They considered themselves the House of Commons for Rhode

---

[1] Democracy in America, I, 87 (Reeve's translation).
[2] Records, II, 191.   [3] *Ibid.*, II, 223.   [4] *Ibid.*, 445.

Island, and were not slow in claiming some of the most important prerogatives of the English body. On Nov. 6, 1672, it was enacted " that noe tax nor rate from henceforth shall be made, layd or levied on the inhabitants of this Collony without the consent of the Deputys present pertaining to the whole Collony." In the preamble the reason for this legislation is set forth. It is declared that " the House of Commons is the peoples representatives there, and the Deputys the representatives of the freemen here ; " and as no tax can be levied in England without the consent of the House of Commons, so, too, is it equally just that tax legislation for the colony should meet the approval of the deputies.[1] The power of the deputies was further increased by another act of the same date providing that no law concerning the " King's honor " or " the peoples antient right and libertys " should be passed without the presence of " the major part of the Deputys belonging to the whole Collony." It was added that any act of the nature indicated, passed contrary to the above provision should be " voyd and of none effect." [2]

The deputies had now attained some of the most important attributes of the bicameral system, but it is plain from the course of events that they were to be satisfied with nothing less than complete separation. On May 6, 1696, they express their desire by way of formal resolution " that it may be made an act of this Assembly, and pass as a vote of the house, that all the Deputies of each respective town, shall sit as a House of Deputies, for the future, and have liberty to choose their Speaker among themselves, and likewise the Clerk of the Deputies ; and that the majority of the Deputies so assembled, shall be accounted a lawfull House of Deputies." [3] This was agreed to, and the Governor and Council were constituted the upper house of the Assembly.

---

[1] Records, II, 472-3.   [2] *Ibid.*, 473.   [3] *Ibid.*, III, 313.

CHAPTER II.

THE MIDDLE COLONIES.

Section I.—New Jersey.

The first legislative Assembly that ever convened in New Jersey was bicameral; and, though this was in apparent contradiction to the terms of the charter, and notwithstanding the fact that strenuous efforts were made to revert to a single-chambered legislature, the system was never abolished. The colony was organized under the *Concessions*[1] of February 10, 1665. By this instrument the government of the colony was vested in a legislative body composed of a governor, a body of councillors, not less than six nor more than twelve in number, and twelve representatives or deputies chosen by the "ffreemen or cheife Agents to others of the Province." The Governor was to be appointed by the Proprietors and the Council by the Governor. Thus councillors and deputies came to be regarded at once, and rightly so, as the conservators of the interests of the Lords Proprietors and the people respectively. To this fundamental difference were largely due the early introduction of the bicameral system and much of that discord which characterized the legislative proceedings of New Jersey throughout the entire colonial period.

---

[1] "THE CONCESSIONS and Agreement of the Lords Propriators of the *Province* of *New Cesarea* or *New Jersey* to and with all and every the *Adventurers* and all such as shall settle or plant there." New Jersey Archives, I, 28–42. Leaming and Spicer's "Grants and Concessions," etc., 12–26.

27

It is reasonably, though not absolutely, clear from the language of the *Concessions* that the Proprietors intended that the Governor, councillors, and representatives should constitute a General Assembly of one house. This seems plain from the fact that the Governor or Deputy-Governor is designated as the presiding officer of the legislative body constituted as above indicated. The phraseology is, however, indefinite and at times ambiguous; and it was obviously to the advantage of the councillors to avail themselves of this ambiguity and to insist on sitting apart from the deputies, since the increasing growth of the colony would soon cause the deputies far to outnumber the councillors.

It was not until April 7, 1668, that the Governor issued a call for an assembly. The burgesses were directed to choose " able men that are freeholders " to join with the Governor and Council "in the Management of affaires." [1] In obedience to this call the first legislative Assembly of the colony was convened on May 26, 1668. The councillors immediately insisted on sitting by themselves, and contended that such an arrangement was in harmony with the evident intention of the *Concessions*. The fact, however, that there were ten deputies present and only seven [2] councillors had, no doubt, considerable weight in bringing them to this conclusion. It must have been plain that in any instance when the interests of the Proprietors were opposed to those of the people—and such instances were certain to arise—the councillors would be outvoted by the deputies. It seems plain, too, that the Council was impelled in the matter more by an instinct of self-preservation than by any conscientious scruples regarding the interpretation of the *Concessions*. To become a legislative nonentity was not a pleasing prospect. At any rate, they carried their point and the two branches of the Assembly deliberated apart. [3] This meeting lasting but four days seems to have been harmonious.

---

[1] New Jersey Archives, I, 56–7.   [2] Leaming and Spicer, 77.
[3] *Ibid.*, 84.

It was brought to a close at the request of the deputies. They sent a communication to the Council saying that they had perused certain bills submitted to them by that body but asked that final action be deferred until next meeting. To this the Council assented. At the next meeting held on Nov. 3, 1668, it became evident that the differences between the two branches of the Assembly were, for the time at least, irreconcilable. The deputies were not to be easily reconciled to the bicameral arrangement, and the councillors seemed intent on thwarting the popular advantage to be gained from an assembly of one house. Early in the session, Nov. 6, 1668, the deputies express themselves to the Council thus : " We finding so many and great Inconveniences by our not setting together, and your apprehensions so different to ours, and your Expectations that Things must go according to your Opinions, though we see no Reason for, much less Warrant from the Concessions, wherefore we think it vain to spend much Time of returning Answers by writings that are so exceeding dilatory, if not fruitless and endless, and therefore we think our way rather to break up our meeting, seeing the Order of the Concessions cannot be attended unto." [1] In reply to the above the Council request the deputies to appoint two of their number to confer with them regarding the alleged infringements of the *Concessions.* " If reason will satisfy you," the reply continues, " we shall be very well pleased that you proceed according to the Lords Proprietors Concessions and the Trust imposed upon you, if not you may do what you Please, only we advise you to consider well of your Resolutions before you break up." [2] Such correspondence as this, however, was hardly conducive to arbitration ; consequently on the following day, November 7, the Assembly adjourned not to meet again for seven years. As might be expected the colony drifted rapidly toward anarchy. A rival government was set up under the leadership of James Carteret, and deputies elected by the popular party met at

---

[1] Leaming and Spicer, 90.   [2] *Ibid.*, 90–91.

Elizabethtown on May 14, 1672,[1] and proceeded to act as the lawful Assembly of New Jersey.   In this critical juncture prompt action was indispensable for the preservation of the authority of the Proprietors.   Philip Carteret the Governor and James Bollen, Secretary of the Council, proceeded at once to England and laid the whole matter before the Lords Proprietors.   Inasmuch as the *Concessions* of 1665 had been the object of such bitter contention, and since that instrument had been so differently interpreted by the Governor and Council on the one hand and the deputies on the other, it seemed incumbent upon the Lords Proprietors to declare the "true intent" of the disputed clauses.   This they did in an instrument bearing the date December 6, 1672, and styled, "A DECLARATION of the true intent and Meaning of us the LORDS PROPRIETORS, and Explanation of there Concessions made to the Adventurers and Planters of New-Caesarea or New Jersey."[2]   It is clear from a perusal of this document that its title is a misnomer.   It is not a "declaration of the true intent and Meaning . . . . and Explanation of the Concessions" but a very essential modification of that fundamental instrument. The effect of this *Explanation* was to enhance very materially the power of the Council at the expense of the General Assembly as a whole.   The Proprietors, naturally enough perhaps, favored the Council in their exposition of the mooted clauses.   It is evident, too, that they were induced more by expediency than by considerations of abstract justice or by a logical construction of the terms of the *Concessions.*   The "explanation" of most importance for our present purpose is the declaration regarding the deliberations of the General Assembly.   "WE the LORDS PROPRIETORS," they affirm, "do understand that in all Generall Assembly's, the Governor and his Council are to set by themselves, and the Deputies or Representatives by themselves, and whatever they do propose to be presented to the Governor and his Council, and upon

---

[1] New Jersey Archives, I, 89–90.   [2] *Ibid.,* I, 99.

their Confirmation to pass for an Act or Law when Confirm'd by us." [1] Whatever may have been the intent of the *Concessions* of 1665, the above is clearly a declaration for the bicameral system.

On Nov. 5, 1675, a meeting of the General Assembly was held after an interval of seven years. Although the sessions were now regular it was evident that the new dispensation was not at all satisfactory to the deputies. The attitude and temper of the two houses are clearly disclosed in the correspondence [2] which took place between them at a meeting from Oct. 19 to Nov. 2, 1681. The deputies objected to the *Explanation* of Dec. 6, 1672, on the ground that it curtailed their power to the advantage of the Council, and further contended that the *Concessions* of 1665 should " be taken according to the Letter w^{th}out any Interpretacon whatsoever." They characterize the *Explanation* as " a Breach of the Concessions " and "desire and Expect that the same' may be made voyd and of none effect." They state in their communication to the Council that their action is not hasty or ill-advised, but that on the contrary they have " perused and well weighed " the contents of the document under consideration. To this the Council submitted the somewhat tart rejoinder that if they " had alsoe the Benefitt of understanding," they " would neither have desired nor Expected the same to be made voyd." They declare it " a matter of lamentac'on that the Representatiues of this Province should be soe shorte sighted that they cannot see that he which runnes may Read." A joint meeting is

---

[1] New Jersey Archives, I, 100–101. The *Explanation* also granted to the Governor and Council the power "to appoint the Times and Places of meeting of the General Assembly, and to adjourn and summon them together again : " a power formerly vested in the General Assembly as a whole. New Jersey Archives, I, 99.

On July 31, 1674, Sir George Carteret in a body of " *Instructions* " to the Governor reiterates the *Explanations* of 1672, thus proclaiming again the bicameral system. New Jersey Archives, I, 167–175. Leaming and Spicer, 55–67.

[2] New Jersey Archives, I, 354–365.

proposed for discussing the points at issue. Failing in this, recourse is again had to pot and kettle correspondence. The crisis came on Nov. 2, 1681. On that day the Clerk of the Council appeared in the House of Deputies at the head of a committee and requested that body to accompany him to the council chamber, there to discuss, and, if possible, settle their points of difference. The Speaker replied that the deputies wished " to consider of it a little." Thereupon the Clerk of the Council declared the " Pretended house of Deputies " dissolved, and left upon the table a letter in which the Council had " freed their minds." The letter charges the deputies with considering themselves the entire Assembly ; and adds that if they were at all qualified to act as representatives they would have good manners enough to prevent them from assuming so much. " It was Lucifers Pride," say the councillors, " that Putt him upon settling himselfe where God never intended to sett him and his Presumption produced or was the forerunner of his fall." The deputies are accused of arrogating to themselves powers never given to them by the *Concessions* or the laws of England. In addition they are twitted with being more zealous for private and selfish ends than for the welfare of the colony. " Private Spiritts in men in publique employ^{mt} are the Jewels that addorne yor brests." " Everything being beautifull in its season and soe we bid you fairewell " is the parting shot from the Council's well supplied magazine of invective. Thus ended in failure the strenuous endeavor of the deputies to revert to the *Concessions* of 1665 and a single-chambered legislature.

In 1683 the Proprietors issued "*The Fundamental Constitutions*"[1] for the government of the province, but attached certain conditions with which the people were to comply before availing themselves of the privileges of the new instrument. Although this new frame of government was not put into operation,[2] it is interesting to note the changes in the constitu-

---

[1] New Jersey Archives, I, 395.   [2] See Mulford's *History of New Jersey*, 219.

tion of the legislature.   The law-making power was vested in a " Grand Council " to be composed of the Proprietors or their proxies and the representatives.   They were to constitute one house, but in voting a distinction was made between the Proprietors and the representatives.   One-half of the Proprietors and one-half of the representatives were to constitute a quorum; and the votes of two-thirds of the representatives and one-half of the Proprietors present at any meeting were necessary for the passage of a bill.   This constitution, then, if put into operation,[1] would establish a peculiar kind of unicameral legislature in which the system of checks and balances so potent in bicameral legislatures would operate.

The legislative Assemblies thus far noticed are those of New Jersey up to July 1, 1676; after that date they belong to the history of *East Jersey*.   On the date just mentioned the province was divided[2] into East and West Jersey by the *Quintipartite* deed.   Although of secondary importance for our present purpose, a brief consideration of the West Jersey legislature is essential.   The fundamental law was comprised in *"The Concessions and Agreements"*[3] of March 3, 1677. The legislature consisted of one house.   The whole province was to be divided into one hundred " proprieties " and the inhabitants of each were to choose one representative.   These " Deputies, Trustees or Representatives " were to constitute the " General, Free and Supream Assembly."   The Assembly met for the first time on November 25, 1681, and for a time continued to meet regularly.   Finally on April 15, 1702, the

---

[1] The reasons why this constitution—which appears in many ways an improvement upon the old form—was not adopted, do not appear in the records.   The Deputy-Governor did not press its adoption, as he was intructed to do, and there were certain features of it not entirely agreeable to the colonists.   See Mulford, p. 221.

[2] New Jersey Archives, I, 205.

[3] " The Concessions and Agreements of the Proprietors, Freeholders, and Inhabitants of the Province of West New-Jersey in America."   New Jersey Archives, I, 241–270.   Leaming and Spicer, 382.

two colonies of East and West Jersey were surrendered [1] to the Crown, united, and made a royal province. Lord Cornbury was appointed to govern both New York and New Jersey, and his commission [2] and *"Instructions"* [3] constituted the fundamental law of New Jersey throughout the remainder of the colonial period. [4] The legislature was composed of thirteen councillors named in the *"Instructions,"* and twenty-four representatives chosen by the people—twelve from East and twelve from West Jersey. The sessions were to be held alternately at Perth Amboy and Burlington—in East and West Jersey respectively. The Council and House of Representatives, following the custom of East Jersey, sat apart. [5]

Another change of some importance was made in the legislature in 1738. In that year New Jersey was separated from New York, and the Governor of New Jersey withdrew from the deliberations of the Council. [6]

---

[1] Leaming and Spicer, 615; Archives, II, 452.

[2] Archives, II, 489. [3] *Ibid.,* 506.

[4] Cf. Gordon's *History of New Jersey*, 54–5.

[5] Journal and Votes of the House of Representatives of New Jersey, p. 21.

[6] Mulford, p. 335. Frothingham (*Rise of the Republic,* p. 20, n.) says that the House and Council sat together. It is plain from the records that they did not. For instance, in the records of the first meeting of the House of Representatives, held in 1703, we find the following entry : "A message from y[e] Council by Maj[r] Sanford, That they have agreed to a Bill Entituled a Bill for Regulating y[e] purchasing of Lands from y[e] Indians, wth some Amendm[ts], to w[ch] they desire the Concurrence of this H[s]." (pp. 20–1, Journal and Votes of the House of Representatives of New Jersey. Other instances of the same tenor appear on the same pages.)

Frothingham further says : "In 1738, the council was made a separate branch ; the governor withdrew from it, and no longer was the presiding officer." (Note, p. 20.) As authority for this statement he refers to Mulford, 335, and herein lies the explanation of the error into which Mr. Frothingham has fallen. What Mulford says is this : "The Council were made a separate branch of the Legislature ; the Governor refraining from *immediate* participation in any measure relating to Legislative proceedings." (History of New Jersey, p. 335.) Mulford evidently does not mean to say that the Council was separated from the House at this time, but that the Governor, who formerly presided over the Council, now withdrew and left that body

Section II.—New York.

For New York the story is quickly told. True to the governmental instincts of the Teutonic race, and inspired by the example of the New England colonies, the people of New York began to move for a representative government immediately after that colony came into the possession of the Duke of York; but the experience of the Stuarts with popular assemblies was not particularly reassuring, and, as a consequence, the request was postponed until it seemed necessary to make the grant for financial reasons. Intimations that the boon of self-government would be granted were forthcoming from time to time. In a letter [1] to a New York officer, under date of Feb. 11, 1682, the opinion was expressed that "his R^{ll} H^s" would "condescend to ye desires of y^t Colony in granting y^m equall priviledges, in chooseing an Assembly &^{c} as ye other English plantations in America" had. The Duke himself expressed a like intention in a letter of March 28, 1682, upon the condition, however, that the colony "provide some certaine fonds for ye necessary support of ye governem^t." [2] The hopes thus raised were soon realized. In the "*Instructions*" to Governor Dongan, issued Jan. 27, 1683, that official was ordered to summon a representative Assembly to join with himself and Council in making laws "fitt and necessary to be made and established for the good weale and governem^t" of

---

of itself a separate branch. Mulford was fully aware that the two houses did not sit together up to this time, as he mentions instances in which bills passed by one house were rejected by the other. "The bill prepared by the committee was passed by the House, and sent to the Governor and Council; but it met the fate of the preceding ones, it was rejected by a majority of the Council." Such is the language of Mulford in speaking of the fate of a bill at the meeting of December 7, 1710. (History of New Jersey, p. 310.) Other examples of similar import appear on the pages of Mulford.

[1] Colonial Documents of New York, III, 317.   [2] *Ibid.*, 317–318.

the colony.[1] Governor Dongan did as he was directed, and on
Oct. 17, 1683, the first legislative Assembly of New York
was convened.[2] It was a bicameral body, the Governor and
Council constituting one house and the representatives the
other.[3] At this meeting a very important act was passed—the
" Charter of Libertys "[4]—in accordance with which the government of the colony was to be organized and administered
under the superior control of the Duke of York. This charter
provided that representatives chosen by the people should,
with the Governor and Council, constitute " the supream and
only legislative power under his Roy[ll] Highnesse." Provision
was made for two distinct houses. It was provided " Thatt
all bills agreed upon by the said Representatives, or the major
part of them," should " bee presented unto the Governor and
his Councell for their approbacon and consent," and that " all
and every which said bills so approved of and consented to by
the Governor and his Councell," should " be esteemed the
laws of the province." The charter was sent to the Duke of
York and approved by him, October 4, 1684.[5] Shortly [6] after

---

[1] Colonial Documents, III, 331.

[2] Journal of the Legislative Council of New York, Introduction, p. XI.

[3] Appended to the first bill of the session—the " Charter of Libertys "—
to be mentioned presently, is found the following memorandum :

"NEW-YORKE, Oct. 26, 1683.

" The Representatives have assented to this bill, and order it to bee sent
up to the Governo'r and Councell for their assent.

" M. NICOLLS, *Speaker.*"

" After three times reading, it is assented to by the Governour and Councell this thirtieth of October, 1683.   THO. DONGAN.

" JOHN SPRAGGE, *Clerk of the Assembly.*"

Brodhead's *History of the State of New York*, II, 661, Appendix E.

[4] The Charter is printed in full in Appendix E of Brodhead's *New York*,
II, 659.

[5] Historical Magazine for Aug., 1862, Vol. VI, p. 233; Chalmers' *Annals*,
I, 588; Brodhead's *New York*, II, 416, n.

[6] March 3, 1685.

241] *The Middle Colonies.* **37**

his coronation, however, he vetoed it.[1]. Governor Dongan was accordingly notified in a body of *"Instructions"*[2] issued May 29, 1686, that the charter was "repealed & disallowed." The law-making power was placed in the hands of the Governor and Council, and the representative body was abolished. The powers of the Governor were more specifically designated in his commission[3] of June 10, 1686. He was empowered "with the advice and consent of" the "Council or the major part of them, to make, constitute and ordain Laws, Statutes and Ordinances for the publick peace, welfare & good Government"[4] of the province. All such laws, however, were to be sent to England for royal approval within three months after their passage. In obedience to these instructions Governor Dongan dissolved the Assembly, January 20, 1687.[5]

The government of the colony thus devolved upon Dongan and his Council of five. This form was continued, under Andros as well, until Leisler took the government in his own hands in 1689. At his call an Assembly met in April, 1690, and again on September 15, of the same year. Both of these consisted of two houses. News of the usurpation was immediately sent to England,[6] and, on November 14, 1689, a commission[7] was issued to Henry Sloughter to be Governor of the colony. By this commission the representative Assembly so ruthlessly brushed aside by James II in 1685, was revived. The Governor was empowered "with the consent of" the

---

[1] Colonial Documents, III, 357.

In a document entitled "Observacôns upon the Charter of New York," and bearing the same date as the veto, are set forth various reasons for withholding, or rather withdrawing, the royal assent. It is urged among other things that the charter "seems to take away from the Governor and Councill the power of framing Laws as in other Plantations." This observation is made upon that clause which provides that bills passed by the representatives should be presented to the Governor and Council for their approval. Colonial Documents, III, 358.

[2] Colonial Documents, III, 369.   [3] *Ibid.*, 377.   [4] *Ibid.*, 378.

[5] Journal of the Leg. Coun. of New York, Introduction, XVII.

[6] Colonial Documents, III, 585.   [7] *Ibid.*, 623.

"Councill and Assembly or the major part of them," "to make constitute and ordain Laws Statutes @ ordinances for y⁰ publique Peace, welfare and good Government" of the province.[1]   This commission with some slight modifications formed the fundamental law of New York until the Revolution.[2]   The first session of the legislature was held on April 9, 1691.[3]   The two houses sat apart, the Governor presiding over the Council.[4]   In 1736, however, it was declared "inconsistent" for the Governor to sit and vote as a member of the Council; hence he withdrew, and it was made a standing rule that the oldest councillor present should preside.[5]

Section III.—*Pennsylvania and Delaware.*

These two colonies may well be treated together inasmuch as the organic connection between them was not totally severed until the Revolution.   Both were governed under the same colonial charters, and it was not until a comparatively late period that the bicameral system was introduced into their legislatures.

The first charter of government for Pennsylvania was that granted by William Penn on July 11, 1681.[6]   This may be dismissed at once since it makes no provision for a legislative body.

The second "frame of government"[7] was granted on April 25, 1682, and by it a legislative body was constituted consisting of a Governor, Council, and General Assembly, the two latter

---

[1] Colonial Documents, III, 624.

[2] Cf. Thompson's *History of Long Island*, I, 168.

[3] Smith remarks that the laws passed by this Assembly were the first ones deemed valid by the courts.   History of New York, I, 98, n.

[4] The Governor and Council were appointed by the Crown.   Colonial Documents, III, 623.

[5] Journal of the Leg. Coun. of New York, XXIX.

[6] "Certain Conditions, or Concessions," etc.   Charters and Constitutions, II, 1516.   [7] *Ibid.,* 1518.

bodies being chosen by the people. The Council was to consist of seventy-two members and the Assembly of two hundred.[1] The Governor or his Deputy presided and had a "treble voice." The power of initiating legislation was in the hands of the Governor and Council. It was their duty to " prepare and propose" bills to be affirmed or rejected by the Assembly. Penn had given the science of government much and serious thought, and this mode of legislation seems to have been his favorite scheme. He would revert to the old Greek method of having legislation prepared in a *boulê*. Such a system, however, is not in harmony with Teutonic instincts and traditions, and a short space of time served to demonstrate the fact that the people would. insist upon originating legislation in their popular assemblies. It should be added, however, that in this scheme of Penn's some provision was made for amendment by the Assembly. For the first eight days of the session the members of the Assembly were to "confer with one another" regarding the proposed legislation. If they so desired, a committee of twelve from the Council would be "appointed to receive from any of them proposals, for the alteration or amendment of any of the said proposed and promulgated bills." Upon the ninth day of the session the Assembly was to "give their affirmative or negative" to the proposed legislation.

Thus far our narrative has had to do with Pennsylvania alone; but on Aug. 24, 1682, Penn received by deed [2] from the Duke of York that land which has since become known as Delaware. From this time on we find the terms "*Province*" and "*Territories*" used to designate Pennsylvania and Delaware respectively. In the latter part of the same year the Province was divided into three counties—Bucks, Philadelphia, and Chester—and the Territories, likewise, into three—New Castle,

---

[1] These numbers were found to be too large and were afterward reduced.
[2] Proud's *History of Pennsylvania*, I, 201 ; Hazard's *Annals of Pennsylvania,* 1609–1682, 588, 590.

Kent, and Sussex.[1] These "three lower counties" were formally annexed to the Province by an "*act of union*" passed by the first Assembly on Dec. 7, 1682.[2]

The first Assembly under the charter met at Philadelphia on March 10, 1683.[3] In this the counties upon the Delaware were represented.[4] At this session a request was made by the Assembly for a new charter. The request was granted by the Governor, and a new charter drawn up by a committee[5] of six from each body was accepted and signed by Penn on April 2, 1683.[6] This was to constitute a frame of Government for "Pennsylvania and Territories thereunto annexed." The Council was to consist of eighteen and the Assembly of thirty-six, both elected by the people. Although the method of passing laws remained the same in the charter, a very essential change was made in practice. The Assembly complained that their prerogatives were restricted within too narrow bounds by being allowed only to confirm or reject bills, and demanded the right to originate legislation. This idea was embodied in a resolution of the Assembly and was approved by the Governor. Although protests were made by Penn against this privilege, it was exercised at intervals until 1696; at which time it was incorporated in a new frame of government.[7] The Assembly was now for the first time granted the charter privilege of originating bills. Bills passed by the Assembly were to be sent to the Governor for his approval or rejection, "with the advice of the Council."

---

[1] Proud, I, 234.   [2] *Ibid.*, 206; Hazard, 611.

[3] Colonial Records of Pennsylvania, I, 57. The Council met on this date and the Assembly two days later. Cf. Proud, I, 235.

[4] Three councillors and nine assemblymen were chosen from each county, making seventy-two in the entire body. This number was much smaller than that called for by the charter, as it was deemed inconvenient to elect the large number there specified. The Governor approved the change. Proud, I, 237–8.

[5] Colonial Records, I, 69.   [6] Charters and Constitutions, II, 1527.

[7] See Gordon's *History of Pennsylvania*, 79–80, 106; Proud, I, 394–5; Hazard's *Annals*, 609. For this frame of government, see Poore's *Charters*, II, 1531.

Finally on the 28th of October, 1701,[1] the charter was issued which remained in force until superseded in Pennsylvania and Delaware by their respective state constitutions, both drafted in 1776. This charter provided that the legislative power should be vested in a representative Assembly composed of four members from each county. Laws were to be enacted by the Governor with the "consent and approbation" of this Assembly. Penn also, by letters patent,[2] appointed a "Council of state" consisting of ten men, who, among other duties, were to serve the Governor in an advisory capacity. Bancroft says,[3] in writing concerning the government in Pennsylvania in 1754, that the right to revise legislative acts was denied to the Council and that long usage confirmed the denial. This is no doubt legally true, but an inspection of the records reveals the fact that in practice the Council really did amend legislative acts. The Governor had a veto on all bills, and acted with the advice of the Council; hence it was necessary for the Assembly to frame their laws in such a way as to meet the approval of the Governor and his Council. This they did. At a meeting of the Council held January 22, 1749, three bills were sent to the Governor for his approval. Amendments were proposed to all of them, and they were returned to the Assembly.[4] Instances are also cited where the Assembly give notice to the Council that they agree to the amendments proposed.[5] In this legislation the theory differs from the practice. It somewhat resembles the method in vogue at the present time whereby members of Congress ascertain in advance the kind of bill to which the President will give his signature.

Up to the date of the last charter, Pennsylvania and Delaware were governed by the same legislature, with the exception of a period of two years extending from 1691 to 1693. The friction between the two colonies, however, had been all

---

[1] Charters and Constitutions, II, 1536.   [2] Proud, I, 451, n.
[3] II, 397. (Last revised edition.)   [4] Colonial Records, V, 426.
[5] *Ibid.*, 426–7.

but continuous; consequently Penn provided in the new charter of 1701 that the Province and Territories might have separate legislatures in case of continued disagreement. The Territories demanded by virtue of this clause a legislature of their own, and in 1703 an agreement was effected by which their wish was realized. The two colonies retained their distinct legislatures under the same executive until the Revolution. The legislatures, as above noted, consisted of single chambers. In Delaware, the bicameral system was introduced by the constitution of 1776,[1] while in Pennsylvania the legislature consisted of a single house until the adoption of the constitution of 1790.[2] A unicameral legislature was the natural outcome of Penn's ideas of government as embodied in his various charters. Even in her first state constitution, that of 1776, Pennsylvania still clung to the single-chambered legislature. In this the influence of Franklin is apparent. He was in pre-revolutionary days, as Bancroft says, " the soul of the Assembly," and always resisted any change from what he termed the simplicity of a legislature of one house. He was also the President of the constitutional convention which drew up the state constitution of 1776, and then also championed with ability and success the idea of a single house.

---

[1] Charters and Constitutions, I, 273.   [2] *Ibid.*, II, 1548.

CHAPTER III.

The Southern Colonies.

Section I.—Maryland.

It required but five years for the Maryland colony to outgrow the primary assembly and to appreciate the superior efficiency of the representative form. The several hundreds and the Isle of Kent were each instructed to elect deputies or burgesses to represent them at a meeting of the Assembly to be held at St. Mary's on Feb. 25, 1639. This they did, and on the first day of the session an act was passed "For the Establishing the house of Assembly."[1] It was declared by this act that the House of Assembly should consist of the Lieutenant-General, the Secretary of the province, the gentlemen summoned by special writ of the Lord Proprietary, the burgesses, and "such other Freemen (not haveing Consented to any the Elections as aforesaid)." In order not to make the transition from the primary to the representative assembly too abrupt, it was provided that those freemen who wished to do so might refrain from voting and then demand seats in the Assembly. This was actually done in some instances and seats were granted accordingly. The absurdity of the plan was soon seen, however, and it fell into disuse.

It was to be expected that those summoned by special writ would be looked upon as representing the interests of the

---

[1] Proceedings of the Assembly, 1637/8–1664, pp. 81–2. See also Chalmers' *Annals*, I, 213; Bacon's *Laws of Maryland*, 1638, ch. I; Griffith's *Annals of Baltimore*, 7.

Lord Proprietary, and that the burgesses would consider themselves the only true representatives of the people. A strong community of interest sprang up among the burgesses and received emphatic expression in 1642. On July 18 of that year the burgesses, "either actuated by the spirit natural to representatives, or animated by the example of the Commons of England,"[1] desired to sit by themselves and have a negative on the acts of the remaining members of the Assembly.[2] It seems plain that the separation was desired not by a faction of the burgesses but by the entire body. This is evident from the fact that the motion was made by Burgess Robert Vaughan "in the name of the rest." The request was denied, however, by the Lieutenant-General, and for eight years longer the Assembly continued to sit as one house. It is clear that in the meantime the burgesses were becoming exceedingly jealous of their prerogatives, or rather of what they considered their prerogatives. For example, in July of 1642 the Lieutenant-General wished an appropriation for a military expedition against the Indians. The matter met with serious opposition on the part of the burgesses. In the course of the discussion the Lieutenant-General plainly apprises them that it is not his intention to counsel with them upon the advisability of such an expedition, in as much as decision in matters relating to peace and war was vested in him by the patent. In short, he desired to know the amount of their appropriation and not their opinions.[3] It is not the wont of representative bodies, however, to subside under a rebuff from an agent of the king. Royal opposition serves only to consolidate. Consequently, on Aug. 1, of the same year, Mr. Greene, burgess from St. Mary's hundred, objected to the passage of a certain bill on the ground that it was not voted for by the major part of the

---

[1] Chalmers, I, 219.

[2] Proceedings of the Assembly, 1637/8–1664, p. 130; Bacon's *Laws of Maryland*, 1649, ch. XII.

[3] Proceedings of the Assembly, 1637/8–1664, 130–1.

burgesses, although it secured a majority of the Assembly as a whole.[1]   Although the matter was decided against him and the Assembly declared one house, the claim of Mr. Greene, without precedent though it was, is interesting in showing that the line of demarcation between the burgesses and those summoned by special writ was being more distinctly drawn.

The separation was finally effected on the first day (April 6) of the session of 1650, by an act " for the settling of this present Assembly."   It ran thus : " Bee it Enacted by the Lord Prop^r wth the aduise & consent of the Counsell & Burgesses of this prouince now assembled.   That this p^rnt assembly during the continuance thereof bee held by way of Vpper & Lower howse to sitt in two distinct roomes a part, for the more convenient dispatch of the business therein to bee consulted of. And th^t the Gou^r. & Secretary, or any one or more of the Counsell for the Vpper howse." [2]   The burgesses, " or any fiue or more of them " were to constitute the lower house.   The two branches were declared to " haue the full power of, & bee two howses of Assembly to all intents and purposes."   It was further declared that all bills passed by the two houses and indorsed by the Governor should be laws of the province, " after publicōn thereof, ... as fully to all effects in Law as if they were aduised & assented unto by all the ffreemen of the province personally."   From this time on we find the laws of the colony enacted " *By the Lord Proprietary with the advice and assent of the upper and lower house of this Assembly.*" [3]

---

[1] Proceedings of the Assembly, 1637/8-1664, 141.

[2] *Ibid.*, 272–3.   See also, Bacon's *Laws*, 1650, ch. I ; Griffith's *Annals of Baltimore*, 13–14.

[3] Bacon says (*Laws of Maryland*, 1649, ch. XII), that the two houses were separated in 1649.   There is, he says, no record of the act by which this was done, but he argues that the separation must have been made at some time prior to the last day (April 21) of the session of 1649, since the laws passed on that date were enacted "*By the Lord Proprietary, with the Assent and Approbation of the Upper and Lower Houses.*"   The laws of this session as printed in the Maryland Archives, however, purport to have been passed by the Lord Proprietary by and with the consent of the General Assembly, no

Section II.— Virginia.

The account of the introduction of the system into the Virginia legislature must of necessity be brief, since the sources now available do not relate in a satisfactory way the details of the process of the separation of the Council and the House of Burgesses.

In June of 1619, Governor Yeardly issued a call for a legislative Assembly to consist of two burgesses from each plantation, town or hundred. This, the first representative Assembly that convened in America, met in Jamestown on July 30, 1619. The twenty-two burgesses met in one body

---

mention whatever being made of "Upper and Lower Houses." It is true, however, that in the manuscript book of laws (Liber C and W H), from which Bacon drew, we do find the upper and lower houses mentioned in the enacting clauses of laws of April 21, 1649; but the manuscript volume from which the laws were compiled (Liber A), as printed in the Maryland Archives, is older and considered by the editor, Dr. William Hand Browne, to be more reliable than the one used by Bacon. By adopting the reading of the laws as found in the Maryland Archives we are relieved from the necessity of supposing, as Bacon does, that an act was passed separating the two houses in 1649, but that the record of it has been lost. If such an act were passed in 1649, why repeat it in 1650 ? It seems more reasonable to suppose that the copyist of Liber C and W H, used by Bacon must have inserted the reference to the upper and lower houses, without considering that such an expression was not applicable to 1649.

Chalmer's states (*Annals*, I, 219-20), that the separation was made "during the distractions which ensued" in 1649; but since in his account of the colony of Maryland, he leans confidingly upon the arm of Bacon, the origin of his error, if such it be, is apparent.

Hannis Taylor (*The Origin and Growth of the English Constitution*, p. 24) says that the legislature was divided into two chambers in 1647, and refers the reader to Winsor, *Nar. and Crit. Hist. of Amer.*, III, 536, and to Doyle, *Virginia, etc.*, pp. 286–291 for an account of the early Assemblies. The writer in Winsor, Mr. W. T. Brantly, says, however, on the page above indicated that "At this session [1650] there was first made a permanent division of the Assembly into two houses." Doyle, however, says (p. 291) that the separation was made in 1647. In this he is obviously incorrect. C. E. Stevens in his *Sources of the Constitution*, p. 18, copies Taylor's statement, apparently without consulting Winsor.

with the Governor and Council, and so continued to do until 1680. The testimony of Beverley is definite upon this point. " Before the year 1680," he says, " the council sat in the same house with the burgesses of assembly, much resembling the model of the Scotch parliament; and the Lord Colepepper, taking advantage of some disputes among them, procured the council to sit apart from the assembly; and so they became two distinct houses, in imitation of the two houses of parliament in England, the lords and commons; and so is the constitution at this [1705] day." [1] Culpepper seems to have been adroit in playing off one branch of the Assembly against the other to subserve his own interests and further his political schemes. More than once does he appear in this role.

Section III.—The Carolinas.

In the legislative history of the Carolinas there is little that is of importance to us in our present study, since in South Carolina the bicameral system has prevailed from the beginning of the legislative history of that colony, and in North Carolina it is impossible to determine just when or how the system originated.

According to the " *Concessions* " [2] issued by the proprietors in 1665 for the government of North [3] Carolina, the legislative power was vested in a General Assembly consisting of twelve " Deputyes or representatives " together with the Governor and Council. The latter body was to be appointed by the Governor, and was to consist of not less than six nor more than twelve members. This Assembly was to constitute one

---

[1] History of Virginia, 187–8, Campbell's Edition.

[2] Colonial Records of North Carolina, I, 79–92.

[3] It seems convenient to use the terms " North " and "South " but the division between the two was not really made until they became royal colonies.

house[1] over which the Governor or his Deputy was to preside.

The *Fundamental Constitutions*[2] of Locke and Shaftesbury of 1669 provided for a " Parliament" consisting of the proprietors or their deputies, landgraves, cassiques, and popular representatives. They were to sit together in one room and each member was to have one vote.[3] All bills were to be prepared by a Grand Council, and nothing whatever was to be proposed in the Parliament which had not previously been passed by the Council.[4] It was readily seen by the proprietors that this constitution could not be enforced at once on account "of the want of Landgraves and Cassiques and a sufficient number of people;" hence a temporary constitution,[5] embodied in a list of instructions to the Governor and Council, was sent over in 1670 and put into operation. This constitution provided for a unicameral legislature consisting of twenty representatives chosen by the people and five deputies appointed by the proprietors. All laws were to be ratified by the Governor and three at least of the five deputies. Although this Assembly consisted of a single chamber it is not difficult to perceive the germ of the bicameral system in this provision for ratification by the three deputies. It was no doubt from this idea that the upper house was evolved. It is impossible to say just when the separation of the deputies and representatives took place. It was probably a gradual process which received formal recognition in 1691. Since the deputies could defeat any measure by refusing to ratify it, it seems probable that they did not care to attend the sessions of the

---

[1] The language of these "*Concessions*" is almost identical with that of the New Jersey Concessions of Feb. 10, 1665, under which two houses were organized. The Carolina construction of the document seems far more plausible.

[2] Charters and Constitutions, II, 1397.

[3] *Ibid.*, 1404.   [4] *Ibid.*, 1403.

[5] Colonial Records of N. C., 181.

Assembly except when they wished to promote some legislation favorable to the interests of the proprietors.[1]

On Nov. 8, 1691, a body of instructions[2] was issued to Governor Ludwell. This document constituted a new frame of government for the colony. The legislature was now to sit in two houses. The lower house was to consist of twenty representatives, while the landgraves, cassiques and deputies were designated as the upper house.

In 1729 proprietary government in North Carolina ceased with the sale of the colony to the crown, but in the instructions[3] to the royal Governor the legislature of two houses is plainly continued.[4]

The constitution of 1776 provided for a Senate and a House of Commons.[5]

South Carolina had a separate legislature but was under the same Governor with the northern colony until 1712. Sources of information for the early history of the Carolinas are very meager, but it seems clear that the legislature of South Carolina, practically from its beginning, consisted of two houses. Ramsay says[6] that the first legislature assembled in 1674[7] and consisted of the "governor, and upper and lower house of assembly; and these three branches took the name of parliament." The legislative records do not begin until 1682.[8] It seems plain, too, that though the legislature consisted of two houses, it lacked some of the most essential attributes of the bicameral system in its highly developed form. Although no serious attempt was made to put the Fundamental Constitutions into operation as a whole, yet an effort was made to apply some of their provisions. On December 16, 1671, a short set of instructions was framed for Governor Yeamans in

---

[1] See Bassett's *The Constitutional Beginnings of North Carolina*, J. H. U. Studies, Twelfth Series, III, 57–8.   [2] Colonial Records, I, 373.
[3] *Ibid.*, III, 90.   [4] See Sec. 14 of the Instructions, p. 93.
[5] Charters and Constitutions, II, 1411.
[6] History of South Carolina, I, 34–5.
[7] This date is doubtful.   [8] Statutes of South Carolina, I, Preface, iii.

which he was directed to have all legislation prepared in the Council. " For there is noe thing to be debated or voted in y⁰ Parlᵗ., but wᵗ is proposed to them by y⁰ Councill."¹ The popular branch, however, would not consent willingly to have its power thus curtailed, and agitation upon the matter continued until the final settlement in 1694. In that year Governor Smith made the following significant announcement to the Assembly : " The proprietors have consented that the proposing power for the making of laws, which was heretofore lodged in the governor and council only, is now given to you as well as the present council."² " Henceforth," says Rivers,³ " the Assembly claimed the privileges and usages of the House of Commons in England, and the proprietors allowed the claim." Under the royal government the bicameral system was retained.⁴

Under the constitution of 1776⁵ the legislature consisted of two houses, and the Council was chosen by the Assembly. The constitution of 1778⁶ provided for a Senate and a House of Representatives.

Section IV.—Georgia.

The history of Georgia contains almost nothing of importance for our present purpose. The colony was surrendered to the Crown in 1752, and two years later a royal government⁷ was established much resembling that of South Carolina. The legislature was bicameral, as might have been expected ; but in making a state constitution in 1777, Georgia followed the precedent of Pennsylvania and established a legislature consisting of a single house.⁸

In the constitution of 1789, however, provision was made for " two separate and distinct " houses.⁹

---

¹ Rivers' *Historical Sketch of South Carolina*, App., p. 369.
² Rivers, 171. Quoted from MS. Journal of the Commons, May 15, 1694. Also quoted in Winsor, *Nar. and Crit. Hist. of Amer.*, V, 314.
³ p. 171.   ⁴ See Ramsay, I, 95.   ⁵ Charters and Constitutions, II, 1617.
⁶ *Ibid.*, 1621.
⁷ Cf. Stevens' *History of Georgia*, II, 370–389; also Jones' *History of Georgia*, II, 460–487.
⁸ Charters and Constitutions, I, 378, 379.   ⁹ *Ibid.*, 384.

CHAPTER IV.

THE FEDERAL CONSTITUTION.

When the framers of the Constitution met in 1787 many of them were not novices in the science of constitution-making. On May 10, 1776, Congress had " recommended to the respective assemblies and conventions of the United Colonies, where no government sufficient to the exigencies of their affairs " had " been hitherto established, to adopt such government as " should, " in the opinion of the representatives of the people, best conduce to the happiness and safety of their constituents in particular, and America in general." [1] Eleven [2] of the states acting upon this recommendation had adopted new constitutions before 1781. The experience of these four years so prolific of new constitutions could not fail to be beneficial to the members of the Federal Convention, and particularly so from the fact that many of them had been members of the constitutional conventions in their respective states. [3] We are not surprised, then, to find immediate precedents for many of

---

[1] Journals of Congress, Vol. II, 166. The resolution was published with a suitable preamble on May 15. *Ibid.*, 174.

[2] Connecticut prefixed a few short introductory paragraphs to her charter and retained it until 1818. Rhode Island substituted the sovereignty of the Commonwealth of Rhode Island for that of the King and thus retained her charter until 1842.

[3] Nathaniel Gorham was a member of the Massachusetts convention and one of a committee appointed to draft the constitution. Madison was a member of the Virginia convention of 1776. Gouverneur Morris, Jay, and Livingston were appointed a committee to draft the New York constitution of 1776. Morris also took a prominent part in the debates of the convention.

the elements of the Federal Constitution in these early state constitutions. This is especially true in case of the bicameral system. When the motion was made in the Convention that the national legislature should consist of two houses, the delegates from Pennsylvania alone voted in the negative. All of the states except Pennsylvania and Georgia had the bicameral system in their legislatures and naturally favored its introduction into the national legislature. The sentiment in Georgia was evidently in favor of two houses, although she had at the time a single-chambered legislature. The delegates from that state voted with the ˙majority, as we have seen ; and, in 1789, the system, pure and simple, was introduced by her new constitution. It is highly probable, too, that Pennsylvania was in favor of the system, as we find it incorporated in her constitution of 1790. Madison tells[1] us that the delegates from Pennsylvania voted in the negative on this question probably in deference to the opinion of Franklin, who favored a legislature composed of a single house.[2]

The views of the states thus expressed through their constitutions could not fail to attract the attention of the members of the Federal Convention. Colonel Mason, in speaking of the advisability of having the national legislature to consist of two branches, said[3] that he was thoroughly convinced that the American people desired more than one house in their national legislature and cited as proof of his assertion the fact that all of the states except Pennsylvania (and he should have excepted Georgia,[4] also), had incorporated the bicameral system into their constitutions.

---

[1] Elliot's *Debates*, V, 135.

[2] The fact that Congress under the Articles of Confederation was composed of a single house was no doubt largely due to the influence of Franklin. The committee that drafted the Articles based them upon the plan of the same name submitted to Congress by Franklin on July 21, 1775. This plan, of course, provided for a unicameral legislature. The connection between the two documents is evident from a comparison of their texts. For Franklin's plan of 1775, see the Secret Journals of Congress, Vol. I, p. 283.

[3] Elliot's *Debates*, V, 217.   [4] Charters and Constitutions, I, 378.

Of the two opposing plans of government, that introduced by Governor Randolph and familiarly known as the "Virginia Plan" provided for a legislature consisting of two houses; while the plan brought before the Convention by Mr. Patterson, and known as the "New Jersey Plan," advocated a legislature composed of a single house. It must not be supposed, however, that the advocates of the "New Jersey Plan" were of necessity antagonistic to the bicameral system. They believed that the Articles of Confederation should be "revised," "corrected," and "enlarged," and were opposed to the drafting of a form of government either entirely or essentially new. Indeed many of them considered that the Convention would be exceeding its authority by going beyond the mere revision of the Articles. Consistent adherence to this idea would involve the advocacy of a single-chambered legislature such as existed under the Articles of Confederation.

Thus by 1790, the Federal and all of the state legislatures were composed of two houses; and the legislatures of all of the other states upon their admission were similarly constituted, with the single exception of Vermont. Although not admitted until 1791, Vermont formed a constitution as early as 1777. This constitution [1] was an adaptation of the Pennsylvania constitution of 1776. This was due to the influence of Dr. Thomas Young, a man of note and a citizen of Philadelphia. Dr. Young had shown a great interest in the affairs of Vermont and, when in a letter [2] dated April 11, 1777, he recommended [3] the Pennsylvania constitution as a model, his suggestion was speedily adopted. It has been thought that the Vermont constitution was drafted by Dr. Young, but there seems to be no positive evidence upon the matter.

---

[1] Charters and Constitutions, II, 1857.

[2] This letter is printed in Thompson's *Vermont*, pt. II, 106.

[3] "This constitution," says Dr. Young, "has been sifted with all the criticism that a band of despots were masters of, and has bid defiance to their united powers." Thompson's *Vermont*, pt. II, 106.

The constitutions of 1786 [1] and 1793 [2] continued the single-chambered legislature, but an amendment to the latter, adopted in 1836,[3] made "the general assembly of the State of Vermont" to consist of a Senate and a House of Representatives.

From 1836 to the present time the state legislatures have uniformly consisted of two houses.

In conclusion, then, we may note the fact that the causes which operated to separate the colonial legislatures into two branches were different in the different colonies; and in most of them there was a gradual evolution of the system influenced either consciously or unconsciously by the English model. This English influence no doubt accelerated the appearance of the bicameral system. It was only six years after the founding of the colony of Massachusetts Bay that the two branches of the legislature were declared coördinate, and after a lapse of fourteen years they were deliberating as well as voting separately.

Our survey of the subject also leads us to conclude that the bicameral system in the Federal Constitution is, in its growth and development, essentially American; but the bicameral principle, the germ and genesis of the institution, must be sought on foreign soil. That there should be a sentiment in the Convention of 1787 all but unanimous in its favor, is not strange when we consider the abundant precedent therefor in the state constitutions, the colonial governments, and more remotely, in the English Constitution. In the gradual evolution of the system we would naturally expect to find it a feature of the Articles of Confederation, and such doubtless would have been the case were it not for the influence of Franklin and the example of the Continental Congress.

---

[1] Charters and Constitutions, II, 1869.
[2] *Ibid.*, 1877.   [3] *Ibid.*, 1883.